Claire Bear, Where Are You?
Ellijay, Georgia

Written by Claire Dieterle
Illustrated by Nancy Garnett Peterson

Copyright © Claire Dieterle 2024

The book's author and illustrator retain sole copyright to their contributions to this book.

Dedicated to Jasper, who loves visits from "Claire Bear"!

Claire Bear, Claire Bear, Claire Bear,
 Where are you, where are you, where?

I'm out in the country and having a wonderful day
In a little town in Georgia called Ellijay.

The word Ellijay is from the language of the Cherokee
It means "place of green things" like the grass and bushes you'll see.

It also means "many waters" and a lot of them are here
Around the rivers and creeks are animals such as deer.

The people in town are the sweetest you'll ever meet,
For them, having visitors come by is quite a treat.

Cute shops can be visited throughout the day
And there are parks in town where the children can play.

There are many restaurants to match any mood.
You can get Asian, Mexican or even Southern food.

The museums are interesting and really topnotch.
   They cover all kinds of legends like the one of Sasquatch.

This is a town many families come to see
 Where there are mountains and lakes and many a tree.

You can hike in the woods and fish on a lake,
Or just enjoy a view when you take a break.

There are many rivers that circle around
The Cartecay and Ellijay rivers join together downtown.

The Coosewattee River has many cool fish
You can catch Trout or Carp or Bass if you wish.

You can visit plenty of farms with many animals there,
 Where you can feed them and milk them and pet their soft hair.

There are chicken farms and goat farms just outside the town,
The goats are many colors like black, white and brown.

This is an apple capital as you may already know,
  There are numerous orchards where the apples do grow.

There are countless apples in the colors green, yellow and red,
Here they sell apple donuts, jellies, fritters and bread.

Carter's Lake is a lovely place tourists go to see.
It was man-made in 1977, by the US Army.

There is skiing and picnicking and also mountain biking.
There is boating and camping and definitely some hiking.

In the South they've got "Lightening bugs" you know
Throughout the night these insects do glow.

There is a variety of animals, like foxes, chipmunks and bats.
Coyotes, deer, beavers, black bears and even bobcats.

The Appalachian Mountains are a beauty you need to see
In Ellijay they surround you as pretty as can be.

The Appalachian Trail is hiked by many every year.
It creates a memory for hikers that they will hold dear.

That is the description of Ellijay, a wonderful town.
People love to visit and drive all around.

When the tourists leave at the end of each day,
"Ya'll come back now, Ya hear!" Is what the people say.

www.ingramcontent.com/pod-product-compliance
Lightning Source LLC
Chambersburg PA
CBHW042052050526
44107CB00109B/1111